PRAISE

"Juliann has written a heart-opening and powerful guide for living life fully through all the challenges and joys. She not only shares her beautiful stories of cycling but then asks the reader to pause and reflect on how her stories give meaning to their own. Her sport is a grand metaphor for how we ride through life. As a master coach, she will expand your consciousness with her insights and questions. Reading *Life Lessons on Two Wheels* will give you both a new perspective of life and of yourself."

— **MARCIA REYNOLDS**, PsyD, MCC and author of the international bestseller, *Coach the Person, Not the Problem* (2nd edition)

"This book will ask you to do the work and to think deeply. It asks you to slow down, look inward, and make intentional choices, and it explains why that is important. Juliann's lessons may have been shaped on two wheels, but their relevance reaches far beyond the ride. As someone who has walked alongside her for many years, learned from her, and been supported by her guidance, I can say with confidence that she is the coach you want for the ride ahead."

— **KARYN EDWARDS**, Ph.D., MCC, Consulting Psychologist, and Founder of Abloom Consulting

LIFE LESSONS ON TWO WHEELS

Life Lessons
on Two Wheels

*An Executive Coach's Guide to
Riding Through Life with
Clarity, Courage, and Choice*

Juliann Wiese, MCC

FOREWORD

My friendship with Juliann has enriched my life. Seeing someone who lives her life with many of the qualities I admire most—presence, resilience, courage, and authenticity—has been a gift.

Juliann and I first met more than 20 years ago, when she was teaching a spin class that my husband and I were devoted to. I had no idea that those sweaty, laughter-filled mornings would lead to one of the deepest friendships of my life, or that we would log thousands of miles together on two wheels. From the very beginning, it was clear that cycling was not just exercise for her; it was a way of thinking, learning, and living.

Together, Juliann and I have ridden the Oregon Coast, climbed and descended the hills of Tuscany, and pedaled across hundreds of miles in Colorado, New Mexico, and Arizona. On those rides, I have watched her push through punishing headwinds, fix flats in the middle of nowhere, laugh through the exhaustion of long climbs, and celebrate the sheer joy of the descent. Cycling isn't just something she does; it is part of who she is.

Cycling has always been her classroom and life her subject matter. That is what makes this book feel so true. What Juliann brings to the page is not theory; it is lived experience translated with wisdom and care into lessons for living life more fully. If you know her, you have witnessed her combination of grit and grace: She will push herself to the edge of what's possible, and then she will pause, reflect, and draw meaning from the experience.

I have also had the privilege of watching Juliann's professional journey. Becoming a Master Certified Coach (MCC), one of the highest and rarest credentials in the coaching world, took more than a decade of disciplined practice, feedback, and growth. Along the way, she also earned a certification in Applied Neuroscience, further equipping her to bridge the science of how we think, feel, and act with the art of how we live and lead. She has taken the same persistence and passion that carried her up countless climbs and poured it into her work with leaders and clients.

In *Life Lessons on Two Wheels*, Juliann combines all of it: the coach, the cyclist, the friend. This book is an invitation to slow down, look inward, and reconnect with the parts of us that too often get buried beneath the noise, pressure, and routine. What makes this book especially powerful is the way Juliann blends her understanding of neuroscience with lived wisdom—explaining not just *what* these traits are but *why* they matter, how they shape our well-being, and how we can cultivate them in everyday life.

This book will both inspire you and challenge you. It will invite you to pause, reflect, and make deliberate choices about how you live. Juliann has spent a lifetime on two wheels, but the wisdom she shares here reaches far beyond the bike. As one of the people who has ridden beside Juliann for many of those miles, I can tell you—she is exactly the guide you want for this ride.

Jodi Tompkins
Board Chair, Lucky Bikes
Denver, CO

TABLE OF CONTENTS

The Ride of Life

When I became an executive coach in 2013, I noticed something interesting. The stories I shared with my clients—the ones that unlocked new perspectives for them—were often born on a bike ride.

The more I reflected, the more obvious it became: My thousands of hours on two wheels had given me more than exercise. They had given me some hard-earned wisdom.

This is not a book about cycling. Yes, there are stories about rides. But this book isn't meant to make you want to ride a bike (although it is great fun!). It's meant to make you want to enjoy your *life* more fully.

Because what I've learned on a bike is that living a full, meaningful life isn't about speed or winning.

It's about:

- **Autonomy**—the joy of choosing your own path.
- **Resilience**—the grit to keep climbing when it gets hard.
- **Presence**—the gift of noticing the moment you're in.

- **Ego**—and the joy that comes when you let it go.
- **Connection**—with people, with nature, with yourself.
- **Joy**—the unfiltered kind, like when you're cruising downhill, bugs in your teeth from grinning too hard.

More Gears

So how do we embrace and practice those aspects of life?

As a coach, I've learned that any significant transformation in someone's life doesn't come from my giving them information or advice; it arrives when they cultivate **new awareness**. When awareness deepens, our possibilities and choices expand—with more options, we can live more fully. A lot like graduating from a tricycle to a ten-speed. More gears, more control, more paths become possible.

Cultivating more awareness means to intentionally grow your ability to *notice*—both what's happening inside of you and around you—without immediately reacting, evaluating, or judging. It's a process of expanding your consciousness so you can see yourself more clearly and respond in ways more aligned with what you want for your life and hope for your future. Here are three ways I'm encouraging you to dial up your awareness through the exploration of this book:

1. Internal Awareness (Self-Awareness)

This is about tuning into your *inner world*:

- Thoughts: Noticing your mental chatter, assumptions, and habitual narratives.
- Emotions: Recognizing what you're feeling in real time, without suppressing or exaggerating.
- Body: Paying attention to physical cues (tension, fatigue, energy shifts) that signal stress or alignment.
- Motives and Values: Understanding *why* you do what you do—the needs or fears that drive behavior.

Cultivating internal awareness helps you move from *autopilot* to *choice* so you can act with intention instead of impulse.

2. External Awareness (Context & Others)

This is about being awake to your *environment*. Understanding the broader context, looking at the big picture rather than focusing on the minutiae. When you expand external awareness, you become more observant; you have more options and a wider range of actions to explore.

3. Meta-Awareness (Awareness of Awareness)

This is the ability to *notice that you are noticing*—a reflective stance that allows you to step back and observe your own mind.

It's what mindfulness and meditation cultivate: the capacity to witness your experience without being swept up in it.

Reflectors On

As a Master Certified Coach (MCC), with 3,000+ hours coaching executives, leaders, and humans, my fifty years of experience cycling kept showing up as a partner in fostering awareness: my own and others'.

For over twenty-five years, I have specialized in adult learning and organizational and leadership development; in addition, I have many professional certifications including one in applied neuroscience. My expertise in these areas has confirmed what I've *lived* on two wheels cycling: We learn through **experience → reflection** on that experience → then **action** that demonstrates learning, and use of that learning in our next actions.

I believe we are generally good at two-thirds of these processes. Reflection is most often the missing piece. We often conflate reflection with rumination.

Not all thinking about our experience is created equal.

My coaching clients often say, "I've been thinking about this problem nonstop." But what they're usually describing isn't helpful **reflection**—it's ineffective **rumination**. These mental models could not be more different; naturally, our brains seem to default to rumination. Research suggests that we think at least 70,000 thoughts per **day**, most of which lean toward worry, doubt, and often inaccurate predictions. The brain is a prediction machine. Neuroscientists call this the **negativity bias**—your brain is designed to scan for potential threats.

Here's more about the distinction:

- **Rumination** is like a hamster wheel. You go in circles, stuck in the past, getting nowhere but frustrated, anxious, and drained.
- **Reflection** is more like a bike ride. You move forward, learning as you go, sometimes uphill, but always toward a new perspective.
- **Rumination** is destructive, looping endlessly about what's wrong, what's missing, or what you fear. Thinking repeatedly until there is no value or learning.
- **Reflection** is productive, pausing to examine, learn, and gain clarity.
- **Rumination** is staring at the hill ahead and convincing yourself you'll never make it. Filling your narrative with negative self-chatter and noise.
- **Reflection**, on a bike, means checking your cadence and adjusting your gears. It's purposeful. It's born of curiosity for learning and adjusting. Its essence is the discovery of options you didn't see before. It's perspective expansion.

Neuroscience backs this up. When you ruminate, your brain loops in what's called the **default mode network**, amplifying stress and self-criticism. Cortisol, a stress hormone, rises, cognitive flexibility drops, and you feel stuck. Your prefrontal cortex is not functioning optimally, and this area is essential for clarity and logical thinking. Reflection, by contrast, engages your **prefrontal cortex, where problem solving flourishes**, which calms your central nervous system and opens new pathways and connections. The result? Clarity, creativity, and emotional relief.

Think of it this way: **Rumination digs the rut deeper; reflection helps you ride out of it.** (BTW, the word *rumination* comes from animals like cows—yes, cows are ruminants like deer and elk—animals that chew their regurgitated food repeatedly. Kind of gross. Don't do it.)

This is why, as an executive coach, one of my goals is to redirect my clients away from the cud-chewing, spiraling, not helpful (not fun either) cycle of rumination toward the energizing momentum of reflection. The table below is one I often use to illustrate the difference—and why choosing reflection changes everything:

FEATURE	RUMINATION	REFLECTION
Focus	*Problem-oriented, past events*	*Growth-oriented future*
Emotional tone	*Negative and self-critical*	*Neutral to positive, curious*
Outcome	*Increased distress, paralysis*	*Insight, clarity, emotional relief*
Cognitive flexibility	*Low*	*High*
Cortisol (stress hormone)	*Elevated*	*Regulated*

Research backs up these theories about rumination vs. reflection. For example, Harvard Business School professor **Francesca Gino** studied how reflection impacts learning and performance. Her research validates: **We get better not just by doing, but by pausing to think about what we did.**

In one experiment with employees in a training program, Gino and her colleagues found that participants who spent just **fifteen minutes at the end of each day reflecting** on what they learned performed **23 percent better** after ten days than those who didn't. The difference wasn't more effort or more practice—it was the power of structured reflection. Our brains are prediction machines. When we stop and reflect, we help the brain update its "models" of what worked, what didn't, and what to try next.

Without reflection, experience can slip past us without leaving a trace. With it, we capture the lesson and strengthen the neural connections that turn knowledge into wisdom.

It's like cycling: If you never pause to look at your route, check your cadence, or notice how your body feels, you might keep repeating the same mistakes. Reflection is the pit stop that makes the rest of the ride more efficient, sustainable, and rewarding.

This book is intended to be your guide to intentional reflection.

Inner Coach

Another way to describe what I hope for you, the reader, is to discover your inner coach—that wiser, kinder, grounded voice within you. The one who believes in your potential and helps you navigate setbacks with grace.

Your inner coach doesn't shout or shame. It asks questions like these:

- *What might I not be seeing yet?*
- *What's another way to look at this?*
- *What do I need most right now?*

As you read, try letting that voice lead. Let it get louder than the critic.

Because self-coaching isn't about fixing yourself; it's about knowing yourself more deeply—your patterns, your values, your capacity to adapt and grow. Fulfillment doesn't come from having a perfect life; it comes from being present and curious enough to live the one you already have.

If you're reading this book, chances are you're already curious about something—yourself, your life, your purpose, or maybe why certain patterns keep repeating. That's a great place to start, because curiosity is like a gearset on a bike; it's the machine of change.

If I've learned anything about change, I've learned that awareness always precedes action. You can't change what you can't see. Self-coaching begins when you slow down enough to ask, *What's really happening here?*

That's where curiosity comes in. Curiosity is also the antithesis of judgment.

Our brains are wired to judge quickly. It's an ancient survival mechanism—scanning for threats, deciding what's safe or unsafe, right or wrong, good or bad. But that same snap judgment can keep us stuck when it comes to growth. When something uncomfortable arises—a mistake, a feeling, a setback—our mind jumps to *What's wrong with me?* instead of *What's here for me to learn?*

Curiosity and judgment can't coexist. One closes, the other opens. Judgment shrinks the space for possibility; curiosity expands it.

Children are naturally curious. They fall a lot, touch things, ask *why* endlessly, and rarely attach shame to what they don't know. Adults, by contrast, are conditioned to equate not knowing with failure. We think we're supposed to have it all figured out. But growth only happens when we're **willing to not know**—to get curious about what's new, uncomfortable, or uncertain.

So, if I'm right and you're curious, let's lay out the elements for enhancing your reflections, curiosity, and learning:

Our Road Ahead, Together

Each chapter in this book includes a set of stories and insights that form a toolkit: stories to make it real, the reflective questions to make it personal, and science to make it possible.

I hope that what emerges for you is useful, meaningful, and life-affirming.

- **Life Lesson:** These lessons are not unique to me. You don't need to be a cyclist to understand them. The lessons can help everyone.
- **My Story:** I'll share my experiences on the bike that led to my personal insights.
- **Neuroscience of the Ride:** Insights to show you why the lessons are validated and significant for growth and change.
- **Client Story:** I'll share how the lessons show up in life outside of the cycling connection.

- **Your Coaching Reflection:** Here I've laid out the questions for you to reflect upon. Get curious about yourself; give yourself time to reflect on who you are and who you want to be. Slow down in this section.
- **Tools:** Here I've given you some ideas for alternative and additive ways to explore activities that may expand your awareness and learning from each of the life lessons.
- **Action:** These are suggestions for ways forward to experiment with and to see what amplifies your learning.
- **Closing Thought:** Ideas I want to share that resonated with me.

Applying Neuroscience

I began integrating neuroscience into my coaching and writing because research over the past few decades has changed how we understand ourselves. It provides practical tools for living, not merely theoretical frameworks for academia. For a long time, the popular belief was that the brain worked like a machine: Emotions "came from" certain parts, decisions were the result of logic battling feeling, and habits were like hardwired circuits. Simple, but not quite true.

Consider scientists such as Lisa Feldman Barrett, whose work on the constructionist theory of emotion has reshaped how we think about feelings. Instead of being automatic "hardwired" reactions, emotions are something your brain *constructs* in the moment. They're predictions, built from your past experiences and the data your body is sending right now. That's why two people can face the same situation—say, riding down a steep hill on a bike—and one feels exhilarated while the other feels terrified. The difference isn't in the hill; it's in how each brain predicts and constructs that moment. This perspective is powerful because it means you're not just at the mercy of your emotions. By training your awareness, practicing new habits, and providing your brain with fresh evidence, you can rewire how you feel and respond.

Other researchers have contributed practical insights, too:

- **Edward Deci and Richard Ryan**, creators of *Self-Determination Theory*, showed that motivation thrives when three needs are met: autonomy (having choice), competence (feeling capable), and relatedness (feeling connected). These ideas show up in everything from how we work to how we parent.
- **Antonio Damasio** demonstrated that emotions and reason are not opposites but partners. Your body and brain work together to guide decisions, and without feelings, logic alone doesn't carry you far.
- **Daniel Kahneman and Amos Tversky**, though psychologists by training, illuminated the brain's shortcuts and biases—why we jump to conclusions, why we overestimate risks, and why we sometimes make choices that aren't in our best interest.

All these thinkers—and many others—have helped move neuroscience out of the lab and into everyday life.

What used to sound abstract ("the brain is plastic") now translates into practical truth: *You can change, you can learn, you can build new neural pathways, habits, and patterns at any age.*

As you read this book, consider yourself both the rider and your own coach. This is your chance to explore your own terrain: the patterns, stories, and strengths that shape your ride through life.

So, let's get ready to start pedaling. The ride is waiting.

CHAPTER 1

Presence Is Precise

*Happiness, not in another place but this place . . . not
for another hour, but this hour.*
—WALT WHITMAN

Life Lesson: The Power to Create Your Future
Starts in the Present Moment

My Story: On the Handlebars with Dad

My dad is the reason I have a love affair with cycling.

My earliest memory—or more likely one shaped by the
stories my parents told me—is of riding to kindergarten
perched on the handlebars of his bike. We were living in
San Francisco, California, in the late 1960s. My dad had
just bought himself a Schwinn ten-speed for $100, and off
we went: a little girl with her daddy, pedaling a few blocks
to school. Not the safest thing to do with a preschooler,
but times were different then, and I remember it feeling

very special. It represented togetherness, connection, and shared experience.

Those moments with my dad set the course for a lifetime relationship with bicycles. My dad rode into his late 60s, often taking week-long touring trips alone, with friends, or with my brother. He modeled something essential for me: Do the things that make you happy, expand your perspective, and challenge you.

Following in his "bike tracks," I've been in love with cycling for more than 50 years.

I'm in my 60s now, still cycling, both road and mountain biking. I've ridden in foreign countries, including epic tours across Canada, Ireland, Spain, and Italy. I've done five century rides (100 miles or more), and I've accumulated thousands of miles in the saddle.

One of the most significant things riding a bike has taught me is that my best life isn't lived worrying about the future or regretting the past. It's lived in the present moment.

Riding a bicycle requires presence. You can't check out if you are in traffic or daydreaming on a technical descent. You can't lose focus when you are climbing over rocks and roots and flying right next to a big, nasty cactus. You must pay attention. And when you do, you get the bonus of noticing other things in your environment. The smells along the way (not all of them good). The sense of the weather: wind, heat, and humidity as it shifts, the grade under your legs, the sheep on the road. In Ireland, there were a lot of sheep on the road.

On a bike, you don't just pass through the world—you *join* it. You are present for what's around you, in front of you, beside you.

While riding with my husband and friends through Italy, Spain, and Ireland, I noticed that the way locals responded to cyclists was different. It wasn't the same as the way they interacted with tourists tumbling out of buses or rushing through sightseeing checklists. When we rolled through their towns and villages on two wheels, the welcome felt different—warmer, more genuine. People smiled, waved, and sometimes even shouted encouragement.

It was as if they recognized that by cycling, we were immersing ourselves in their world at a unique pace. We weren't just passing through; we were experiencing their land, their culture, and their rhythms in a way that honored them. In those moments, I realized something powerful: Moving slowly and with intention changes how we are received. It invites connection.

That's true in life. When we slow down, notice, and engage with presence, people respond differently. They feel seen, they let us in, and we feel there, present.

Neuroscience of the Ride: Why Presence Matters

Lisa Feldman Barrett's constructionist theory of emotion tells us our brains are *prediction machines*. They don't passively record the world—they constantly use past experiences to guess what will happen next and prepare our bodies to act. That's why we so often get pulled toward replaying the past or rehearsing the future. Our brains think they're helping, even though it's not always true. But presence interrupts this unhelpful loop.

When you ground yourself in what you see, hear, smell, and feel right now, you give your brain *new raw data*. On a bike, the terrain shifts so quickly that your brain has no choice but to recalibrate. In life, you can train your brain to achieve the same recalibration through micro-pauses, reflection, and sensory awareness.

Presence isn't just peace of mind. It's a neurological reset—an upgrade to how your brain constructs reality.

Presence isn't just peaceful; **it's precise.**

Client Story: Rushing Through Life

One of my executive clients was the picture of success. She was leading a large division of a travel management company, constantly in motion, her days packed from dawn until late at night. In one of our sessions, she lamented how fast everything was moving, the endless number of meetings and work. Almost under her breath, she said, "I don't remember what I did yesterday; it all blurs together."

From my perspective, she was living her life like she was sprinting to some undetermined grand finish line—rushing from one thing to the next, worrying about tomorrow, constantly revisiting and ruminating about what had gone wrong yesterday and what wasn't done. I sensed she wasn't ever fully present.

When I asked, "What are you enjoying about your work?" she looked at me like, "Are you kidding? Nothing!"

We paused. I asked her to slow down her breathing to see what arose. She was visibly shaken. I could feel the tension before the tears showed up. It was clear that pausing was unfamiliar and uncomfortable and that something was emotional for her. She described her life at the time as being on a bullet train where you can't see any of the scenery; you can only feel the pull toward the destination. And now, in the pause, she realized there were things worth slowing down to see. *Ahhh.*

She and I started experimenting with what we termed "micro-presence." Building in some small breaks, maybe just five minutes a day, before her next meeting. We brainstormed on other ways to bring her into the present. She decided not to check her phone as much and instead to look out the window to notice the color of the sky and the day's weather. We also talked about breathing.

The Science of the Breath: Regulating Your Ride

When we feel stressed, anxious, or emotionally flooded, our bodies react long before our minds can make sense of it. The heart rate spikes, the chest tightens, the jaw clenches—these are signals that the sympathetic nervous system (our "fight, flight, or freeze" response) has taken over.

The antidote lies within one of the simplest, most powerful tools we possess: the breath. Your breath is the remote control for your nervous system. Slow, intentional breathing activates the **parasympathetic nervous system**, often called the body's "rest and restore" mode. When this system engages, heart rate and blood pressure drop, muscles loosen, and the brain receives the signal that you are safe.

This is not abstract; it's biology.

Each time you exhale slowly, you stimulate the **vagus nerve**—the longest nerve running from your brain stem through your lungs, heart, and digestive system—which acts as a brake pedal for stress. The longer and slower your exhalation, the stronger the signal that says, *You can calm down now.* When you're on a bike, you know the feeling: The climb steepens, your heart races, and your breathing turns shallow. If you panic, the climb feels impossible. But when you focus on deep, steady breaths—in through the nose, out through the mouth—something changes. Your rhythm returns. Your muscles follow your breath's lead. The same applies to life.

Presence isn't just a mindset; it's a physiological state. You can't think your way into calm—you can breathe your way there.

My client and I worked on the following breathing techniques:

1. **Box Breathing (4x4x4x4)**
   - Inhale for 4 counts
   - Hold for 4 counts
   - Exhale for 4 counts
   - Hold for 4 counts
   - Repeat for 3–5 cycles

(Great before a meeting, a ride, or any moment you feel tense.)

2. **Extended Exhale**
   - Inhale for 4 counts
   - Exhale for 6–8 counts
   - Repeat for 1–2 minutes

(Ideal for activating the parasympathetic system and calming the body quickly.)

She also developed a technique of waiting to respond after counting to 10 in conversations with her colleagues.

Together, we explored using a journal to write down what she was observing because of these small changes.

At one of our later sessions, she mentioned that she had started to be more aware of moments of connection, gratitude, and even joy in the middle of her demanding days. Presence can help you to not take things for granted.

Your Coaching Reflection

Pause here. Breathe. Reflect.

- Are you rushing through your present life because you're always on the way to something else?
- Are regrets about the past or anxieties about the future stealing your attention and joy for living?
- What do you notice when you fully engage in this moment?
- What is one small thing you can be grateful for right now?

Tools: Building the Discipline of Presence

Micro-Pauses: Before meetings, conversations, or tasks, take three deep breaths to reset.

Transition Rituals: When shifting activities, pause for 30 seconds to stretch, notice your body, or set intention.

Presence Cues: Put reminders where you'll see them—a sticky note that says "Now" or "Look Up."

Reflection Journaling: Each day, jot down one moment when you were fully present and describe what shifted.

Single-Tasking: Choose one daily activity (e.g., lunch, walking the dog, brushing your teeth) to perform without multitasking.

Reframe as Training: Presence is not a personality trait—it's a skill you can practice like any other.

Action: Practice Presence

This week, choose one simple place—maybe your commute, a walk, or even making coffee—and treat it as practice in presence. Notice the details. Smell, sound, touch. Let the moment sink in because the truth is that our ride through life is shorter than we think.

Closing Thought: Corny, maybe, but it feels so true: the journey matters as much as, if not more than, the destination. And, often, happiness can be found not at the end of the road but while noticing the road itself—right here, right now.

The present moment is the only time
over which we have dominion.
—THICH NHAT HANH

CHAPTER 2

Freedom and Choice

Happiness is independence.
—Susan B. Anthony

Life Lesson: Choose Your Own Ride

My Story: The Chrome Ten-Speed

For my 13th birthday, I got my very first ten-speed bike. It was brand new. Chrome. Sleek. Mine. That bike wasn't just transportation—it was liberation. My Chrome Mustang.

We were living in Banff, Alberta, Canada, at the time, in the 1970s. It was a magical place: elk, deer, moose, coyotes, and, yes, bears in our backyard and sometimes on the streets, tourists in the summers, long, quiet winters. Banff was enchanting.

The Chrome Mustang made it that much better because suddenly I could go:

- To Fenland Lakes or the Cave and Basin hot springs
  to look for frogs and tadpoles.
- To the Banff Springs Hotel swimming pool.
- To friends' houses scattered across town.
- To the baseball diamond.
- To the river.
- To the fairgrounds.
- To Bow Falls.

When I wanted to go.

No waiting for Mom or Dad to drive me.

With both parents working, my brother and I had hours of unstructured time. With the Chrome Mustang, that time became mine to design. I felt in control, and the world felt full of possibilities. I felt invincible—like I could outrun anything (though, note to readers: you should never run from a bear).

That first bike gave me speed, freedom, and, most importantly, choice. What mattered most wasn't where I went—it was that *I got to choose where and when I went.* That bike was more than chrome and gears; it was my first real encounter with **autonomy**.

I loved the thrill of deciding what to do with my day, where to go, and the simple joy of independence. I got to test my abilities and strength riding up hills and cruising down the other side.

Psychologists Edward Deci and Richard Ryan call autonomy a **core psychological need** in what they call Self-Determination Theory. Autonomy and its expression shape who we are. Autonomy isn't just about doing whatever you want. It's about having the ability to choose, act, and learn from the consequences of those choices. Autonomy offers us dignity, provides agency, and ignites motivation. Without it, we can stagnate.

But here's where mindset enters the ride: We can fully embrace autonomy only if we believe we are capable of growth. If we fall into a **fixed mindset**—believing we're stuck with whatever skills we have right now—we'll shy away from risks, avoid failure, and miss the opportunity to expand our learning.

One way I like to describe a fixed mindset to my clients is that the brain can narrate a "distorted story," ultimately designed to keep us safe—but these stories can also keep us small.

They sound like this:

- *"Don't risk it. You'll fail."*
- *"You've tried before; it didn't work. Why bother?"*
- *"If you were really talented, this wouldn't be so hard."*

Sound familiar? These stories are the brain's way of protecting you—but they're distortions and lies.

Neuroscience and psychology tell us that our brains are

endlessly adaptable. **Neuroplasticity** means we can grow, change, and learn at any age. Stanford psychologist Carol Dweck calls this the **growth mindset**: the belief that effort, persistence, and learning matter more than innate talent.

When we believe in growth, autonomy becomes a gift. We're free to experiment, to try, to fall and get back up—because every ride, no matter how wobbly or challenging, makes us stronger.

Autonomy Is Fuel
Self-Determination Theory: Why It Matters

Self-Determination Theory (SDT)

SDT says that human beings thrive when three basic needs are met:

Autonomy—the feeling that you have choice and control. You're steering your own handlebars, not being forced into a route you didn't choose.

Competence—the sense that you can handle the terrain. You may not always fly up the hill, but you trust that you have the gears, skills, and strength to make it.

Relatedness—the connection with others who matter to you. It's the difference between riding alone into a headwind and sharing the draft of a peloton, supported and encouraged by companions.

When these three needs are satisfied, motivation flows naturally. You don't have to grit your teeth to keep going; you want to keep going. You feel energized, resilient, and capable of more than you thought possible. But when one or more of these needs is blocked, the ride becomes more difficult.

- Lack of autonomy feels like being stuck on a ride you didn't choose and don't like.
- Lack of competence feels like spinning your wheels on a climb you know you can't crest.
- Lack of relatedness feels like pedaling into the strongest headwind without anyone to share the load.

Why does this matter for you as a reader? Because every story and reflection in this book ultimately connects back to one of these needs. The lessons I've learned on two wheels—about presence, resilience, joy, ego, and risk—are about strengthening autonomy, building competence, and deepening relatedness.

Think of SDT as the "fuel mix" for a meaningful ride. Too much of one and too little of another throws things off balance. But when autonomy, competence, and relatedness are in harmony, the ride isn't just about reaching the finish—it's about delighting in the journey.

Neuroscience of the Ride: The Power of Choice

Your brain doesn't just record the world—it **constructs** your experience of it. When you make even a small choice, your brain encodes agency: *I matter. I have control. I can act.* That sense of autonomy boosts dopamine, strengthens motivation, and creates resilience. On the Chrome Mustang, every ride reinforced a new model of myself: capable, free, strong, and independent.

The opposite is also true. Too much of life is dictated by what others say or want for you, thereby training the brain to experience helplessness, fatigue, resentment, and apathy. That's why even micro-decisions—what route to take home, what to eat for lunch, when to pause—matter more than we think. They are small but powerful signals that your life is, at least in part, your own. Autonomy isn't just freedom—it's a neurological power source.

Client Story: Rediscovering Choice

Another client came to coaching because, as he described it, he felt trapped. As a senior leader in the tech industry, his calendar was crammed with commitments he didn't feel he had chosen. His language reflected it: "I have to . . . I can't . . . They expect me to . . ." He was successful, but his sense of freedom had eroded.

In one session, I asked: "Where in your life do you feel like you actually have choice?"

He paused for a long time, then smiled wryly: "Honestly? Only when I'm choosing my lunch."

I asked how that realization was impacting him in other ways. He mentioned that he was feeling resentful, like nobody gave him any credit for having ideas of his own. Like he was a puppet in his life. It felt pervasive, he said, as if the work environment had started to trickle into his home life; he noticed an apathy for things he used to love spending time doing.

He needed a turning point.

Remember that awareness precedes choice. My client was seemingly aware of the lack of his autonomy. So we started small: identifying choices he did have, even in structured situations—how to approach a project, whom to mentor, which meetings to attend in person versus virtually. He noticed that autonomy wasn't all or nothing. It could be reclaimed in small, intentional ways.

Six months later, he was fully in the action phase, taking a bigger step—redesigning his role to focus on the work he found most energizing and in support of the strategic vision he held for his role and his longer-term career.

He told me: "For the first time in years, I feel like I'm steering my own ship again." That's what autonomy gives us: the power to choose our direction, even when the path has constraints.

Autonomy isn't just about freedom—it's also about boundaries.

Many of us equate independence with the ability to say yes to everything, to handle it all, to be capable, flexible, and endlessly available. But as William Ury reminds us in *The Power of a Positive No*, the real strength of autonomy lies in knowing when—and how—to say *no*.

Saying no isn't rejection. It's protection. It's how we preserve our energy, integrity, and focus for what matters most. Each time you say no to something that is misaligned in your life, you are actually saying *yes* to something deeply important—your values, your priorities, your health, your relationships, your sense of purpose.

We live in a culture that rewards busyness as a badge of honor. But when we try to do everything, we end up doing nothing well. Boundaries are not barriers; they're guide rails that keep your life on course. Without them, your autonomy is at risk—because choice without clarity can quickly become chaos.

A well-timed, confident *no* shows you are setting boundaries and creates prioritized space, self-respect, and clarity—for both you and the other person. When you choose what you'll give your energy to, you reclaim authorship of your life. **Freedom, in its truest form, isn't about doing more. It's about doing *what matters most.***

Your Coaching Reflection

Pause here. Breathe. Reflect.

- How are you spending your days?
- Do your daily choices align with your deepest values?
- Where in your life could you increase autonomy, competence, and relatedness?
- When was the last time you felt invincible, free, alive? What were you doing?
- What small choice could you make today that reconnects you with that feeling?
- Where do you feel stuck, dictated to, or trapped in a fixed mindset?
- What "fairy tale" does your brain tell you that keeps you small, afraid, or limited?
- How might you rewrite that story into one of learning, persistence, and growth?
- Where might saying *no* open the door to a deeper *yes*?
- What boundaries protect your sense of autonomy?

Tools: Building Autonomy in Daily Life

Choice Audit: Write down your daily routine. Circle what you freely choose. Star what feels imposed. Adjust one.

Small Wins: Practice autonomy in micro-choices—your route, your order, your next meeting format.

Energy Check: Notice when you feel most alive. What choice enabled that moment? Replicate it.

Boundaries as Autonomy: Saying *no* is often the clearest way of saying *yes* to your values.

Redesign Workflows: Where do you feel like a passenger in your own life? How could you grab back the handlebars?

Rewrite the Fairy Tale: Catch one self-limiting story you tell yourself. Write down its opposite and practice saying it aloud.

Take a Risk: Do something new where failure is possible. Frame it not as success/failure but as practice/learning.

Inventory of Growth: Reflect on three times you've learned something new in the last five years. Let that evidence reshape your story.

Action: Make One Decision

This week, reclaim one area of your life where you've given up choice—big or small. Make one decision that aligns with who you are and what you value most. Because autonomy isn't just about the freedom to ride anywhere. It's about the courage to ride *your way*.

Closing Thought: When we align our choices to our values, there seems to be a noticeable lightness in our being. It's congruent; it fits us. Our choices matter.

How we spend our days is, of course, how we spend our lives.
—ANNIE DILLARD

CHAPTER 3

Heartbreak Hill

Adversity does not build character; it reveals it.
—JAMES LANE ALLEN

Life Lesson: You can do hard things.

My Story: My First Century Ride

Over 2,000 cyclists gathered in Santa Fe, New Mexico, as the desert sun just began to climb over the horizon. It was May, and it was cold. We were at 7,000 feet above sea level. I could smell chain oil, sunscreen, and the faint dust in the high desert air. Some of the riders looked intimidating to me, sleek jerseys and shaved legs, chatting casually like this was just another Saturday spin. Me? I was anxious. I was freaking out that I was about to spend the next eight hours of my life sitting on a bike saddle pedaling 100 miles in one day.

This was my first **century ride**. My husband, who had conquered multiple rides this long and longer, had assured me, "You'll be fine, just pace yourself." Easy for him to say. For him, a century wasn't a big deal.

The first 30 miles passed for me with some excitement and anticipation. My legs felt ready; I was with a group of friends and hoping that we would have some fun along the way. And then, just ahead, looming like a massive brick wall, came the infamous **Heartbreak Hill**.

At mile 35, an 18 percent grade, and the hill that every rider was acutely aware of. I observed cyclists of all levels dismounting and walking their bikes, shoulders slumped. Others tried to grind it out, legs barely moving, their bikes wobbling all over the road, faces contorted in effort. My own brain lit up with panic: *There's no way. Who do you think you are? Just get off and walk like everyone else.*

But something in me said no. I dropped into my lowest gear, stood up on the pedals, and started grinding. My lungs screamed, my quads burned fire, and sweat stung my eyes. Every fiber of my being begged me to stop. And then—almost without realizing it—I crested the top.

I had done it. I had climbed Heartbreak Hill.

And it wasn't just about conquering a hill. It was about proving to myself that I could do something my body, my brain, and even the crowd around me had deemed impossible. That moment reframed not just the rest of the ride for me, but the way I saw myself beyond it.

Growth Requires Discomfort

Here's the truth: Doing hard things feels uncomfortable. Whether it's cycling uphill, changing a habit, or having a tough conversation, your brain will try to talk you out of it. Comfort is safe, familiar, and easy. Discomfort feels like danger. But without discomfort, there is no growth. This is exactly why so many of us set goals—eat healthier, exercise more, sleep better—and then fall off track. Our brains are wired to crave certainty, safety, and immediate gratification. When the going gets tough, we rationalize:

- *"Just this once won't hurt."*
- *"I'm too tired today."*
- *"It's not that important."*

But here's the kicker: Every time we abandon a goal and rationalize the choice, we're training our brains to expect failure. We wire the pattern deeper.

Neuroscientist Donald Hebb put it simply: "Neurons that fire together, wire together." If you repeatedly link quitting with self-justification, that's the circuit your brain strengthens. The way out? Rewire it—by staying with the discomfort long enough to build a new pattern.

Heartbreak Hill is more than a climb; it's a mirror.

If you always choose the easy path, you'll never discover how strong you really are. When you attempt something hard, something that scares you or stretches you, you reveal a deeper truth about yourself. You discover capabilities you didn't know were there. Hard things strip away excuses, bravado, or comparison. You're left with the raw truth of your own resilience. You have it in you. You may not have surfaced it. Yet.

What if the thing you've been avoiding—the "hill" in your life—is the very place where you'll discover your untapped strength?

Neuroscience of the Ride: Struggle and the Constructionist Brain

From a constructionist lens, as mentioned earlier, your brain doesn't simply "record" the challenge—it *predicts* what it thinks will happen based on experience. That's why Heartbreak Hill looked so impossible at the bottom. My brain was protecting my **"body budget,"** overestimating the cost of the climb and underestimating my resources.

But here's the power: When you do the hard thing anyway, you update the model. You give your brain new data: *I can*. That evidence gets stored as embodied memory, so the next time you face a hill—whether on the bike or in life—your brain predicts capacity instead of collapse.

Each struggle you endure becomes a deposit in your resilience account. Neuroscientists call this **prediction error**: Your brain expected failure, but reality delivered success. Over time, those prediction errors accumulate into confidence, grit, and adaptability. Avoid the hill, and your predictions remain rigid. Face it—even imperfectly—and your brain literally rewires to anticipate strength instead of fragility.

What Is a "Body Budget"?

Think of your brain as your body's **financial manager**—but instead of dollars, it manages energy. Every action, thought, or emotion is like a deposit or withdrawal from your **body budget**.

- **Withdrawals** happen when you face stress, lack sleep, push yourself physically, worry, or spend hours in back-to-back meetings. Your brain predicts you'll need more fuel and spends from your body's reserves—raising your heart rate, releasing stress chemicals, and burning energy.
- **Deposits** come from rest, good nutrition, movement, laughter, connection with people you care about, and moments of presence. These recharge your system and give your brain more resources to work with.

  When your body budget is in the red (too many withdrawals, not enough deposits), you feel drained, impatient, anxious, or even sick. When it's in the black (balanced or surplus), you feel clearer, more resilient, and ready to take on challenges.

BODY BUDGET DEPOSITS	BODY BUDGET WITHDRAWALS
Rest & Sleep	*Lack of Sleep*
Good Nutrition	*Poor Nutrition*
Movement/Exercise	*Overtraining/Exhaustion*
Laughter	*Stress/Worry*
Social Connection	*Isolation*
Moments of Presence	*Back-to-Back Demands*

Here's the kicker: Your brain is constantly predicting whether you'll have enough in your budget to handle what's ahead. That's why even *thinking* about a stressful event can make you feel exhausted—it's like your brain is writing a check in advance. So, managing your life well—through rest, presence, autonomy, and connection—is about **managing your body budget wisely**. It's not self-indulgence. It's smart brain economics.

Client Story: A Corporate Heartbreak Hill

While coaching an executive client, I felt like I recognized the exact look I must have had at the base of Heartbreak Hill. She had just been promoted into a stretch role leading a major reorganization.

"This is too big," she confessed. "I'm not sure I can do it. Everyone is watching, and I feel like I'm about to fail in front of the whole company."

Her "hill" wasn't asphalt and altitude—it was visibility, responsibility, and fear of failure. Just like me on Heartbreak Hill, her brain was predicting collapse before she had even started the climb.

While big-picture thinking can help us broaden our view beyond the many details in our lives, sometimes taking a micro-view is useful to reduce cognitive overload. Breaking things down into small efforts. We worked together to do just that. Instead of trying to conquer the entire reorganization at once, she identified her first "gear shift": mapping her team's current state. Then another: clarifying decision rights. Then another: scheduling early listening sessions with her stakeholders. And so on.

Each step built confidence. Each success updated the narrative. She didn't just get through the climb—she redefined what she was capable of as a leader.

That's what Heartbreak Hills do. They reveal us.

Your Coaching Reflection

Take a pause. Breathe. Reflect.

- What's the "hill" in your life right now—the thing that feels too steep to attempt?
- What is your brain predicting about that hill? Is it exaggerating the cost?
- What slight gear shift could you make to start climbing?
- Who could draft with you—support, mentor, or coach?
- How would your self-image change if you made it to the top?

Tools: Pedaling into Hard Hills

Hard things can overwhelm us if we treat them like one massive climb. Instead, try these practical "gear shifts":

Downshift → Break the challenge into smaller gears. Instead of "I have to finish the reorganization," shift to "I can hold three listening sessions this week."

Drafting → Let others help. Cyclists save up to 30 percent of their energy by drafting behind another rider. Who can you tuck in behind for perspective, resources, or encouragement?

Stand and Climb → Push in short bursts. When the hill feels endless, commit to the next 30 seconds. Then the next. Micro-effort builds macro results.

Reframe Discomfort: When the struggle shows up, remind yourself: *This is the feeling of rewiring. This is growth.*

Catch Rationalizations: Write down the excuses you use most often. Replace them with a growth-focused mantra like *I choose my future success over my immediate comfort.*

Celebrate Small Wins: Each step forward is new evidence your brain can store in its resilience library.

Action: Define Your Summit

What's your current "Heartbreak Hill"? Commit to three gear shifts you will make this week to get to the summit.

Closing Thought: A Hill Reframed

For five years, I returned to Santa Fe for that century ride. And every year, Heartbreak Hill was waiting. The dread never completely went away. But something shifted. Each climb added to my resilience library. My brain no longer screamed, *You can't!* Instead, it whispered, *You've done this before. You can do it again.*

The hill didn't get smaller. I got stronger.

So will you.

The best rides are the ones where you bite off much more than you can chew and live through it.
—DOUG BRADBURY

CHAPTER 4

Obstacles and Distortions

Ego is the enemy.
–Ryan Holiday

Life Lesson: Comparison is the thief of joy.

My Story: Everyone Is Faster, Stronger, "Better"

For decades, the bike has been one of my greatest sources of joy and freedom. I own six, each with its own story and purpose. My road bike—a sleek Cervelo—has carried me through many of my touring rides and rides over 25 miles, a trusted partner on countless adventures. Two mountain bikes live in the lineup: one a rugged dual suspension with disc brakes built for technical trails, the other a hardtail that's lighter and more responsive on climbs. I keep two cruiser bikes for slower days—perfect for short spins to the store, a pub, or a meander around the neighborhood. And then there's my Eliptigo, a quirky favorite that lets me ride standing up, part exercise, part joyride. I spent 15 years teaching spinning classes, logged thousands of miles on roads and trails, and climbed mountain passes in some incredible places. Anyone who steps into our garage can see it instantly—with my six bikes and my husband's five, our passion for riding is pronounced.

And yet, for all those miles and moments, there were times when the joy vanished. Not because of the bike. Not because of the amount of climbing. Not because of the weather. Not because I was tired or hungry.

Because of my ego.

I remember leading a spin class one Saturday morning. The room was packed, bikes humming in rhythm, sweat dripping, music pounding. From the instructor's perch, I should have felt confident. I knew what I was doing. Instead, my mind was somewhere else, measuring myself against the riders in the room. Sometimes I was out of breath, sometimes I wanted to get off the bike and give the instructions from the sidelines. Sometimes I heard this voice in my head that said, *They know you're not that fit. They know you're faking it.*

The same thing happened on some of our weekend group training rides. My husband could climb hills with a grace that seemed effortless. He was always at the front, sometimes miles ahead. Many of my friends often dropped me on the climbs. I couldn't keep up. Not on my best days. I would glance at their backs and feel frustration tightening my chest. It ruined the ride for me. I was simultaneously resentful and full of shame.

And here's the hard truth: When my ego was in charge, I was miserable. I was not fun to be around either. I was taciturn and cantankerous. Every pedal stroke felt like a mantra: *You're too slow. You're not fit enough.*

I was completely in my own head, and it was a convoluted, messy place. I wasn't present to the beauty of the day or the camaraderie of friends. I was trapped inside a prison of comparison—of my own making.

Our in-our-own-head monologue (self-talk), if left unchecked, is the breeding ground for many malformed or destructive thoughts. Our brains are master storytellers, constantly spinning narratives to make sense of what we see and feel. The problem is that those stories are often riddled with distortions.

Cognitive distortions are habitual ways of thinking that twist reality and fuel the voice of the ego. They're shortcuts the brain uses to predict and protect, but they often backfire, leaving us anxious, defensive, or small. When our inner narrator runs unchecked, it can sound convincing—but it's not always telling the truth.

Here are a few of the most common distortions:

- **All-or-Nothing Thinking:** *If I'm not the best, I'm a failure.* Ego thrives on extremes. But real life lives in the middle—where effort, learning, and nuance reside.

- **Mind Reading:** *They must think I'm incompetent.* We act on assumptions about others' thoughts, even when most people are too absorbed in their own inner chaos to notice.
- **Catastrophizing:** *If I make one mistake, it's all over.* Ego confuses risk with ruin. The brain's negativity bias magnifies threats, making small bumps feel like cliffs.
- **Discounting the Positive:** *Sure, that went well—but it doesn't count.* The ego loves to move the goalpost, keeping us in a loop of "never enough."
- **Personalization:** *If something went wrong, it must be my fault.* This distortion ties our self-worth to outcomes and denies others' roles in the equation.

What's fascinating—and freeing—is that neuroscience confirms how these distortions form. The brain's **default mode network** is designed for prediction, not accuracy. When it lacks complete information, it fills in the gaps—usually with fear, doubt, or self-criticism.

That's why our internal world can feel chaotic: It's a swirl of half-truths and assumptions masquerading as reality.

The antidote isn't to silence the mind. It's important to notice the noise without believing every thought that rides through. When we slow down, breathe, and observe what's happening in our minds, the distortions start to lose their grip.

The next time your inner voice insists you're behind, unworthy, or alone, pause and ask: *Is that true?* Often, it's just the ego trying to protect you from a discomfort that isn't dangerous.

When we learn to question our thoughts instead of obeying them, the chaos quiets. What remains is clarity, presence, and peace—the place where joy lives.

My ego was thriving in this chaos, telling me these distorted stories:

- *You're not enough unless you are the fastest.*
- *Others are better, so you shouldn't be leading anything.*
- *If you're struggling, it must mean you don't belong in this group.*

Once I stopped comparing myself, allowing myself to ride at my own pace and look around at the scenery, I felt happy that I was out there, doing it. When our group finished the ride, even if I was the last one to finish, we all connected over the shared yet individual experience.

Someone will always be faster than you.

The ego wants to make life a competition.

But the truth I've learned repeatedly is this: Ego erases enjoyment. It steals connection, gratitude, and presence.

Joy comes when you let go of comparison and ride your own ride.

Neuroscience of the Ride: The Comparison Trap

From a **constructionist brain perspective**, emotions like envy, shame, or pride aren't fixed—they're predictions your brain makes. When you see someone ride faster, your brain doesn't simply record speed; it interprets it: *That means I'm behind. That means I don't measure up.* Comparison narrows your focus, activates stress chemistry, and keeps you in threat mode.

Here's the good news: You can retrain your predictions.

Gratitude and connection activate a different circuit. When you shift attention from *scarcity* (*I'm behind*) to *sufficiency* (*How lucky am I to be here, riding with friends?*), your brain constructs a calmer, more expansive experience. Same road. Same climb. Completely different reality.

I like the phrase "words make worlds." With a simple language change, when I stopped asking, *Who's faster?* and instead said, *Look at this sunrise,* I rewrote my own experience. The ride didn't change. My brain's construction of it did.

Client Story:
The Executive Who Couldn't Stop Comparing

One of my clients, a newly promoted executive, embodied this struggle. He had earned his position through talent and hard work, yet almost immediately, he began comparing himself to his peers.

"They're more polished in meetings."

"They have Ivy League backgrounds—I don't."

"What if they realize I don't belong here?"

My client's ego, disguised as imposter syndrome, hijacked his energy.

He second-guessed every decision. He tried to mimic his colleagues rather than lean into his own strengths. Over time, his team began to feel it too—hesitation, lack of trust, and low confidence.

In coaching conversations, I take what's called a **strengths-based approach**.

A strengths-based approach in coaching is a philosophy and methodology that focuses on identifying, developing, and leveraging a client's *natural talents, core values, and existing capabilities*—rather than concentrating on weaknesses or deficits. It is grounded in the belief that people achieve greater growth and fulfillment when they understand and intentionally apply what they already do well.

How It Looks in Practice

A strengths-based coach asks questions like these:

- "When have you felt most energized and effective at work?"
- "What comes easily to you that others might find challenging?"

- "What values or talents are you expressing when you're at your best?

Here are some examples of strengths-based approaches:

Focus on what's right, not what's wrong

I help clients notice and amplify the patterns of thought, feeling, and behavior that lead to success, instead of analyzing deficiencies. This builds energy, confidence, and intrinsic motivation.

Assume potential and resourcefulness

I hold all my clients as *creative, resourceful, and whole*—a fundamental stance in coaching. I know my clients have the internal resources to solve their own challenges.

Build confidence through evidence

By exploring "when you were at your best" moments, I help my clients identify the conditions and behaviors that led to their prior successes. This creates a foundation for replicating success in new contexts.

With my "comparing" client, we redirected his habitual musings toward strengths-based questions and conversations about what was true, namely:

His ability to listen deeply, to engage with others authentically, and to create an environment where people felt seen and valued. That was his unique leadership gift—not polish, not pedigree, but presence and connection.

When he began to focus on his strengths instead of everyone else's, something shifted. His confidence grew. His team responded very positively. He leaned on what he was good at, and it brought both satisfaction and results.

Your Coaching Reflection

Take a pause. Breathe. Reflect.

- Where in your life are ego and comparison stealing the potential for you to feel joy?
- At work, do you measure your progress against others instead of yourself?
- In friendships, do you downplay your worth because someone seems "ahead"?
- In family life, are you chasing unspoken standards that keep you stuck in "not enough"?
- What would it feel like to ride your own ride, without comparison?
- What steady actions could help you build confidence instead of chasing it?

Tools: How to Get Ego Off Your Wheel

Gratitude Sprints

When comparison arises, name three things you're grateful for *in this exact moment.* (On the bike: the view, your legs working, the friend beside you.)

"My Lane" Mantra

Before meetings, conversations, or rides, say: *I ride my lane. My pace is enough.*

Evidence Log

Write down one win every day, however small. Over time, this becomes proof—earned confidence that ego can't erase.

Celebrate Others

When tempted to compare, encourage the "faster rider." Genuine celebration rewires the brain from scarcity to connection.

Joy-Ride Ritual

Schedule one activity each week (a ride, a walk, a meal) where the only goal is joy—not speed, not outcome, just being.

Rewrite the Story

Keep a short journal. When ego steals joy, write a counter-story rooted in sufficiency and presence.

Action: Let It Go

For one whole week, focus on letting go of comparisons. Live your life, ride your pace.

Closing Thought: Ego will always whisper. But you don't have to listen. When you release comparison and practice thinking about your thinking, you free yourself to notice what's real. And what's real—connection, presence, laughter, love—was never about being the fastest rider in the first place.

> *When we remove ego, we're left with what is real.*
> *What replaces ego is humility, yes—but rock-hard*
> *humility and confidence. Whereas ego is artificial,*
> *this type of confidence can hold weight. Ego is stolen.*
> *Confidence is earned.*
> —RYAN HOLIDAY

CHAPTER 5

Friction

The moment we stop seeing conflict as a threat, we
begin to use it as information.
—Brené Brown

Life Lesson: Conflict is a learning opportunity.

My Story: The Infamous High Grade

There's a climb outside Denver, Colorado, called **High Grade**.

It's long, steep, and unforgiving. Once you've finished, you're too tired to lift your bike onto the rack. High Grade isn't just a ride—it's a test, and finishing it earns you credibility in the cycling community.

But High Grade isn't infamous just for the climb. It's also known for its *friction*.

The road is narrow, with little to no shoulder. Signs say *Ride Single File*. And yet, with hundreds of cyclists flocking there every weekend, not everyone adheres the rule. To residents navigating the same winding road in SUVs and pickup trucks, this was maddening. Their anger manifested as honking, yelling, and, at times, even tossing tacks onto the road. Cyclists fumed back—at the drivers, at each other. Even other cyclists would get angry—because every rider who broke the single-file rule fed the stereotype that cyclists are entitled, oblivious, and disrespectful.

I've ridden High Grade dozens of times. I've felt the tension in the air, as real as the burning in your quads. Everyone wanted the same thing—safe passage up the road. And yet the clash was unavoidable.

Because it mattered.

For residents, High Grade was home. For cyclists, it was achievement, endurance, and bragging rights. The road carried meaning for both sides—and where there's meaning, there's conflict.

Over these years of coaching leaders, I've learned this truth: Conflict isn't random. It doesn't erupt out of nowhere. It shows up *where something matters.*

Priya Parker, in *The Art of Gathering*, says: **"Conflict reveals relevance."**

If there's no meaning at stake, we don't bother fighting. The very presence of conflict means something matters—whether it's boundaries, respect, achievement, or identity. Avoiding conflict may feel like relief in the moment, but it comes at a cost:

- Unspoken needs
- Unclear boundaries
- Resentment that grows quietly
- Innovation that never happens
- Relationships that stay surface-level

On High Grade, the battle wasn't about single file vs. two abreast. It was about respect, safety, pride, and belonging. At work, it's rarely just about budget, deadlines, or turf wars. It's about identity, values, fairness, recognition, or purpose.

When conflict arises, the mistake is to treat it like a nuisance. The opportunity is to ask: *What does this reveal about what matters most?*

As I've seen in years of coaching executives and teams, **conflict, handled well, is one of the greatest drivers of growth.**

Neuroscience of the Ride:
Why Conflict Feels Threatening

Through a **constructionist brain lens**, conflict feels threatening because your brain is constantly predicting safety or danger. When resources, values, or identities feel at risk, your nervous system construes the moment as a threat—even if the "danger" is just someone disagreeing with you in a meeting. Your body budget shifts. Stress chemistry floods.

Tunnel vision narrows your options. You're no longer reasoning from your prefrontal cortex; you're bracing from your survival brain. That's why both cyclists and residents on High Grade felt so reactive: Their brains were constructing the situation as an assault on what mattered most.

The way through isn't suppression of emotion—it's *regulation*. Slow breaths, a pause, curiosity—these offer your brain new data. They signal: *This isn't a bear in the woods; it's a disagreement I can navigate.*

Our emotions are data. Organizational psychologist **Adam Grant** reminds us that our feelings are valuable signals, not distractions. They reveal whether a workplace or family culture or, in this case, a community culture, is thriving or quietly eroding trust and connection. Suppressing or dismissing feelings often leads to behavioral subterfuge (like tacks being thrown on the road) and misaligned strategies for dealing with problems (like purposely not riding single file).

Grant's research also highlights how emotion regulation—skills like reframing and self-awareness—helps all of us speak up more constructively when friction hits. When we can reappraise a frustrating situation or pause before reacting, we can channel our strong feelings into clarity, creativity, and courage. We learn to manage our emotions effectively rather than mute them, to communicate more openly, and to innovate more freely.

When we understand emotions and conflict as information and relevance rather than interference, we become better riders on challenging roads—able to navigate the friction without losing our balance.

Once again, curiosity prompts the reframe. Instead of *They're against me,* your brain can construct: *They value something I don't yet see.* That shift alone creates new pathways forward.

Client Story: The Leadership-Team Gridlock

I once coached a leadership team that was paralyzed by conflict. On the surface, the arguments appeared to concern scheduling and staffing. The clash ran deeper: Half the team valued history, stability, and predictability; the other half valued innovation and rapid change. They weren't just disagreeing about meetings—they were disagreeing about the future of the organization.

At first, their instinct was avoidance. Meetings ended with eye rolls, resentment, and substantive discussions occurring in "offline" side conversations. But avoidance only delayed the inevitable. When they finally engaged in facilitated dialogue, something shifted. They realized: *This is hard because it matters. We're wrestling with identity, purpose, and vision—not just logistics.*

Naming the relevance turned the fight into a conversation. They didn't eliminate conflict, but they transformed it into a source of clarity.

Your Coaching Reflection

Take a pause. Breathe. Reflect.

- Where in your life are you avoiding a necessary conflict?
- What does the conflict reveal about what matters most—to you, and to them?
- How would your response change if your first move was curiosity instead of offense or defense?
- What boundaries or values are being compromised when you stay silent?
- How might engaging directly—respectfully, curiously— open new possibilities?
- What would change if you saw conflict as relevance, not risk?

Tools: Navigating Conflict with Presence

1. Name the Stakes

Ask yourself: *What's at risk for me here? What might be at risk for them?*

2. Use "Tell Me More"

When someone's heated, resist rebuttal. Try: "Tell me more about why this matters to you."

3. Shift Your State

Before entering a tough conversation, take six slow breaths. This calms your nervous system and widens your range of choices.

4. Reframe the Road

Instead of thinking, *This is a fight,* try: *This is energy around what matters. Can we put that energy to work?*

5. Conflict Contracts

Teams can set norms: how we'll disagree, how we'll listen, and how we'll decide. Just like the "ride single file" rule, agreements create safety.

Action: Take It On

Think of a situation where you have some friction in your life. It could be personal or professional. Imagine that any tension you feel is signaling significance. Write down what you want to happen and the outcomes you hope to achieve through engaging with conflict. Then step into the conversations that have the potential to reveal new ideas and new connections.

Closing Thought: On High Grade, the truth is that both cyclists and residents belong. Both care. Both have valid stakes in the road. Conflict wasn't a sign of failure. It was a sign of relevance. Life is the same.

Conflict means something matters. It's not something to fear—it's an invitation to find clarity. The real danger isn't conflict. It's ignoring it, and then the road becomes unsafe for everyone.

Conflict is the beginning of consciousness.
—M. ESTHER HARDING

CHAPTER 6

Shift Gears

Growth and comfort do not coexist.
—GINNI ROMETTY (FORMER CEO, IBM)

Life Lesson: Change is hard, so is stagnation.

My Story: Leaning into the Shift

I really love mountain biking. It's challenging, and it's peaceful. My husband and I have some favorite rides where we are in the forest on fire roads, and we are the only people out there; it's a bit of adventure and a bit of meditation for me. But my "fat-tire phase" started with trauma.

In my 20s, I road cycled often with a friend. One afternoon, we were descending a steep hill in Calgary, Alberta, at more than 25 miles an hour. He was just ahead of me when, suddenly, he flew over his handlebars and crashed headfirst into the curb. For a moment, I was sure he was dead. His face and scalp were badly cut, and blood was everywhere.

We flagged down a motorist, who rushed us to the emergency room. My friend needed over 100 stitches in his head alone and suffered countless bruises—but miraculously, no broken bones.

The cause? A rain grate set parallel to the road instead of horizontal. His front tire dropped in, and physics did the rest.

Watching that crash traumatized me. I couldn't stop seeing it in my mind. I decided that narrow road tires were too dangerous, too thin to trust. That's when I began what I call my fat-tire phase. On to the trails, off the highways. Single track and forestry roads.

But here's the thing: Fat tires don't remove risk. They trade one kind for another. Off the road, you leave behind traffic, cars, and storm drains—but you meet rocks, roots, ledges, and cacti. The hazards don't disappear; they just change shape. I lost some battles with hazards. I've broken an arm, picked gravel out of my scraped and bruised skin, and cried more than once after misjudging an obstacle or braking too hard at the wrong time.

When I first started mountain biking, I thought my road cycling experience would carry me through. But on the trail, everything was different.

It was humbling. Changing biking technique wasn't optional—it was necessary. I realized the key to mountain biking (and to life): You must be ready and willing to "shift gears."

Complacency and obstinacy against change in life are just as foolish as refusing to shift on a bike. If you don't downshift on a hill, you'll burn out and fall. If you never upshift on the flats, you'll stall your progress. The bike has gears for important reasons—comfort, efficiency, and manageability.

Yet we humans are creatures of habit. In some respects, this serves us well by providing structure, comfort, and efficiency. But it's also one of our greatest obstacles. We become so ingrained in how we think, act, and feel that we no longer see the pattern.

In life, staying in the wrong "gear" looks like this:

- Burning out by grinding too hard without adjusting pace.
- Spinning your wheels in busywork that gets you nowhere.
- Resisting necessary or meaningful climbs because they are uncomfortable and scary.
- Making excuses, being needlessly defensive, resisting change, and stagnating.

Just as the bike was built with gears to help us adapt, life gives us gears too—habits, mindsets, support systems. Change isn't about abandoning what we've learned; it's about adjusting and knowing when and how to shift. Change is hard, and so is stagnation. In life, you will experience this trade-off often.

The question is: Do you notice when you're stuck in the wrong gear, and are you willing to shift despite the effort involved?

Why Change Feels So Hard

Here's the truth: **Change is difficult for humans.** Not changing may be even harder—but our brains are wired to resist it.

- **The Brain Craves Certainty.** Familiar patterns, even unhealthy ones, feel safe. Disruption sparks fear.
- **Comfort Is a Trap.** The status quo feels easier, but it slowly entrenches us in patterns that narrow possibilities.
- **Transformation Requires Disruption.** True change destabilizes before it strengthens. It feels uncomfortable—sometimes frightening—because your brain is rewiring in real time.

That's why so many people back off just when transformation is beginning.

Here's the paradox: **The discomfort you feel in change is proof that growth is happening.**

Neuroscience of the Ride: Why Change Feels So Hard

From a **constructionist perspective**, your brain is a pre-diction machine. Habits are predictions your brain has automated to save energy. When you try to change, your brain resists—not because you're lazy or incapable, but because it's conserving fuel. That "ugh" feeling of discomfort? It's not proof you can't change—it's just your brain flagging metabolic strain.

With repetition, however, the brain updates its model: This new pattern is safe, efficient, and worth retaining. That's neuroplasticity in action—the rewiring that makes change stick. So, like shifting gears on a bike, change is awkward at first—but smoother with practice. Your brain learns fluency over time.

Client Story: The Executive in the Wrong Gear

One coaching client was an executive known for his brilliance and attention to detail. But his team was frustrated—he micro-managed, got lost in the weeds, and slowed everything down. From my viewpoint, he was grinding in the wrong gear.

When I asked him what was hardest about stepping back, he said, "If I'm not in control, everything will fall apart."

This is a common theme for many leaders and humans. We remain stuck in old patterns that we believe serve us and the greater good, even in the face of evidence to the contrary.

Change will **always** feel difficult before it feels natural.

My client needed this reminder. It won't feel comfortable, and yet it will eventually. And it will be better. Just not right away.

He experimented with small shifts: allowing a direct report to lead a meeting, asking questions rather than giving answers, and pausing before diving into details. At first, he described it as feeling clunky and awkward. But slowly, he realized that these adjustments weren't a loss of control; they were gaining momentum. Over time, despite anticipated setbacks, his team thrived, and so did he.

So, like shifting gears on a bike, change is awkward at first—but smoother with practice.

Your Coaching Reflection

Take a pause. Breathe. Reflect.

- Where in your life are you stuck in the wrong gear?
- Which routines feel draining instead of energizing?
- What would one small "shift" look like this week?
- How might you embrace the adjustment instead of fearing it?

- How is staying in the status quo helping you—or hurting you?
- What might you need to let go of to engage differently?
- Who could you align with to help you hold steady in a new gear?
- What would be different if you saw change not as disruption but as momentum?

Tools: Shifting Into Change

Micro-Shifts, Not Overhauls

Instead of changing everything at once, pick one behavior to adjust. Example: listen two minutes longer before responding.

Anchor New Patterns

Tie the new behavior to a cue. For example, each time you log in to Zoom, take three breaths before speaking.

Reframe Discomfort

When change feels awkward, remind yourself: *This is my brain learning a new gear, not proof I'm failing.*

Accountability Riders

Share your change goal with a trusted partner. As with drafting on a climb, accountability makes the transition easier.

Celebrate the Shift

Notice small wins. Each successful change reinforces the brain's prediction: "I can do this."

Action: Track Your Progress

Decide on something you want more of, or less of, in your life. Write down the steps that will help you achieve this. Keep a visual reminder somewhere where you can see it every day. Keep track of even the smallest movement forward and record your progress.

Closing Thought: You don't eliminate struggle by changing; you make it possible to keep moving. Change is hard. But isn't it harder to stay stuck? Shift now. Shift again later. And keep moving forward.

Even after decades of cycling, I still have days on the road or the trail when I have to adapt to something new. Sometimes I misjudge an obstacle or the pitch, sometimes I stay in the wrong gear too long, sometimes I shift too soon. I'm not always fluid and smooth. Every time I take on a new challenge, I must learn something new about what the bike and I are capable of.

If we don't change, we don't grow. If we don't grow,
we aren't really living.
—GAIL SHEEHY

CHAPTER 7

Headwinds and Tailwinds

A smooth sea never made a skilled sailor.
—FRANKLIN D. ROOSEVELT (OFTEN ATTRIBUTED)

Life Lesson: Strength is built in the struggle, and joy is amplified by what we endure.

My Story: The Big Nasty

Not every ride is fun. I've been on some rides where I have been miserable. I've gritted my teeth, cursed, and fought tears as the wind howled or if the length of the ride seemed endless. Many times, I've said out loud and muttered under my breath, "Why am I doing this?" I've been too hot, too cold, too tired, too sore, and just plain wretched.

But one ride stands above them all when I think about being unhappy: The Big Nasty in Moab, Utah. It was the first weekend in October.

The name itself should have been enough of a warning. Halfway up this arduous, never-ending climb, the weather changed from overcast and comfortable to winds exceeding 40 miles per hour and driving sleet. This blizzard swept in, fast and furious. Snow stung my face; my hands and feet were soaked and numb. Hypothermia wasn't just a risk—it was a real possibility.

Hundreds of riders were caught in the storm. I ended up crammed shoulder-to-shoulder with ten other cyclists in the cab of a pickup truck meant for four. Dripping wet, shivering, scared, and exhausted, I once again asked myself, *Why am I doing this?*

And then, just as suddenly, the storm cleared. The sun broke through. The road dried. Everyone climbed back onto our respective bikes. As we descended from the summit, we were treated to spectacular views. Everything around us was covered in a light dusting of white snow; against the towering red rock formations outside of Moab, it was truly unforgettable.

The joy we all felt was amplified by the storm we had just survived. Without the blizzard, I would have enjoyed the descent. But because of the suffering, I *treasured* it.

Life has headwinds and tailwinds.

- **Headwinds** are the setbacks, illnesses, losses, conflicts, and disappointments. They annoy us, drain us, and test us.

- **Tailwinds** are the moments of ease, support, opportunity, and joy.

Brené Brown, researcher and storyteller, has spent decades studying courage, vulnerability, and emotional resilience. One of her most powerful findings is this: **You can't selectively numb emotions.**

When we try to dodge the hard stuff—fear, grief, disappointment—we also dull our access to joy, gratitude, and love. In her book *The Gifts of Imperfection*, Brown writes: "We cannot selectively numb emotions. When we numb the painful emotions, we also numb the positive emotions."

Think of it like cycling into a headwind. You might wish you could block the sting of the cold air, but if you shut down all sensation, you'd also lose the thrill of the tailwind that comes later. Headwinds and tailwinds are part of the same ride. Avoiding struggle might protect us in the moment, but it robs us of depth and meaning.

The truth is, the more willing we are to feel the complicated emotions, the more capacity we build to feel the good ones fully.

Struggle expands the lungs of our emotional life—so when joy arrives, we can breathe it in deeply. We often wish for only tailwinds. But without headwinds, joy has no sharpness or contrast. Headwinds shape us. Tailwinds restore us. Together, they create a fuller, richer life.

Neuroscience of the Ride: Why Struggle Amplifies Joy

Through a **constructionist lens**, your brain builds experiences through contrast. During a headwind (or storm), your "body budget" is taxed—heart pounding, cortisol spiking, muscles primed. Your brain predicts: *"This is hard; this might never end."* When the struggle eases, your brain experiences a **prediction error**: The hardship ends sooner than expected. The relief floods your system with dopamine and serotonin, making joy feel sharper and more profound. If life were all tailwinds, your brain would adapt and flatten the experience into the ordinary. It's the struggle that primes the nervous system to savor relief, gratitude, and joy.

Headwinds and tailwinds aren't opposites—they're partners in constructing meaning.

Client Story: The Leader in the Storm

One of my clients was caught in the middle of a corporate reorganization. Staff were leaving, budgets were being slashed, and pressure from the board was relentless. Exhausted and frustrated, she said to me, "I just want this storm to be over." When you're facing a headwind like that, the last thing you want to hear is, "It'll make you stronger." Sometimes, when people say that, you want to punch them.

As coaches, we must be careful not to reframe too quickly or too dismissively. Growth isn't found in glossing over pain—it's found in acknowledging it fully, without judgment. Clients need to feel seen before they can see new possibilities.

Still, it was also true that her storm held the potential to transform her.

The Power of "And"

Life is rarely *either/or*. More often, it's *both/and*. Multiple, even conflicting, emotions can be true at once. We live in a culture that loves binaries: yes or no, right or wrong, confident or insecure, strong or weak. But life doesn't work that way, and neither do we. You can be confident in your abilities *and* still feel a flicker of self-doubt. You can be grateful for your life *and* long for something more. You can love someone deeply *and* still feel frustrated or disappointed by them. When we reduce our experiences to opposites, we miss the richness in between.

In coaching, I often invite clients to replace "or" with "and." Instead of "I'm either arrogant for having confidence, or I'm unworthy for doubting myself," try "I can be confident *and* humble. I can trust myself *and* still be learning." That slight linguistic shift opens space for compassion, curiosity, and growth. Our minds crave certainty—it feels safe—but real growth lives in complexity. When we allow for layers instead of dichotomies, we make room for wisdom, empathy, and deeper connection.

Life, like a good ride, is full of gradients, undulations, and curves, not straight lines.

A simple tool I teach my coaching clients when we bump into these binary thoughts is this:

Ask yourself, *What is also true?*

- *I feel uncertain about this project . . . and what is also true is that I've led many successful ones before.*
- *I feel scared about this climb . . . and what is also true is that my legs are strong and trained for this.*
- *I feel overwhelmed . . . and what is also true is that I have support available if I ask.*

It's not about ignoring the difficulties or feelings of inadequacy—it's about balancing them with a fuller picture of reality.

Once my client could see her situation through that wider lens, her "storm" started to look different. It wasn't just chaos anymore—it was a proving ground. She began naming the strengths she was building in real time: adaptability, courage, clear communication, and emotional endurance. She emerged with more confidence, resilience, and clarity about her values. The headwind hadn't just tested her—it had trained her.

Your Coaching Reflection

Take a pause. Breathe. Reflect.

- What headwind are you pushing against right now? What strength is it quietly building in you?
- Where are the tailwinds in your life—moments of grace or ease—that you may be rushing past without savoring?
- How could you reframe one current struggle as a teacher, not just a trial?

Tools: Balancing Headwinds and Tailwinds

Name Your Headwinds

Write down the current challenges. When you relabel them as learning, what emerges?

Savor Tailwinds

Keep a "wind journal"—note daily moments of ease, joy, or support.

Practice Contrast Gratitude

When you experience relief after difficulty, pause and say: *This feels good because of what I endured.*

Find Shelter in Community

Just as I found warmth in that crowded truck, entrust people who can steady you when storms hit.

Trust the Rhythm

Remember: the wind always shifts. What pushes you today may carry you tomorrow.

Action: Ride the Wind

This week, choose one current headwind. Instead of resisting it with frustration, reframe it: What strength is it building in me? Then, when a tailwind comes, celebrate it—don't just speed through.

Closing Thought: Both resistance and ease belong in the ride. One makes you strong; the other makes you grateful. Together, they make you alive.

The greater the obstacle, the more
glory in overcoming it.
—MOLIÈRE

CHAPTER 8

Focus Creates Flow

*Your mindset shapes your reality more
than your circumstances do.*
—CAROL DWECK

Life Lesson: Attention is not neutral.

My Story: The Rocks You Stare At

Mountain biking is exhilarating because it's unpredictable. Trails ask for balance, courage, and agility in real time. Some of my most important lessons came when I got it wrong.

Here's the one lesson that changed everything for me: The rocks you stare at are the rocks you hit.

On a ride early on in my mountain biking journey, my eyes locked on a big, jagged group of boulders. My front wheel tracked exactly where my gaze was fixed: straight into the obstacle I wanted to avoid. Down. Ouch. Not fun.

When my focus shifted to the line I wanted to go on, my bike followed, and I learned the pattern.

Another important early discovery: my brain (likely yours too) exaggerated threats from a distance. Twenty feet out, rocks looked like boulders, and climbs looked like impassable walls. I'd talk myself into "I can't" well before I reached the feature I was worried about—only to realize, once I was on it, that I could.

That's when Henry Ford's old line landed: *If you think you can or think you can't—you're right.*

On a bike and in life, belief and attention set your path forward. If you fixate on what you fear, you unconsciously steer toward it. If you focus on the path you *do* want, your energy and outcomes align. Belief and attention are not passive. They construct your reality and guide your behavior. Where you place it determines your experience.

The Power of Focus

Think about how many times you've focused on what's going wrong in your life instead of what's going right. How often have you found yourself predicting the worst-case scenario—only to realize later that it never happened? Doesn't it feel disproportionate?

Our brains are wired for this. Negativity bias, which I mentioned earlier, is an evolutionary mechanism that helps us remain safe by scanning for threats, avoiding danger, and anticipating loss. But what was once a survival mechanism often becomes a mental roadblock. Catastrophizing—expecting the worst before it even unfolds—narrows our attention like a tunnel, keeping us locked on the "big rocks" instead of the clear path around them.

When we shift our focus, we change our direction. This isn't about toxic positivity or ignoring reality; it's about grounding ourselves in what's true and possible rather than what's imagined or exaggerated. Neuroscience tells us that attention literally shapes perception—what we look for, we find. Our brains are wired for **confirmation bias**, meaning we unconsciously seek out evidence that supports what we already believe, while filtering out information that contradicts it. At the same time, our expectations often become **self-fulfilling prophecies**: When we anticipate failure, threat, or limitation, we behave in ways that quietly bring those outcomes to life. When we deliberately move our attention toward options, solutions, and forward motion, our brains follow suit, creating neural pathways that support problem-solving, adaptability, and hope.

On the bike, where you look is where you go. Look too far behind, and you lose your balance. Look ahead, even when the terrain is rough, and your body naturally adjusts to stay upright. Look down, go down. Life works the same way. The moment we redirect our focus from what might go wrong to what could go right, we stop steering toward the crash—and start riding toward possibility.

Neuroscience of the Ride: Focus and Prediction

From a **constructionist brain perspective**, your brain doesn't simply "see" the trail. It predicts meaning from sensory data. When you fixate on a rock, your brain predicts danger, tightens your body, and primes you for impact. Ironically, that tension steers you into the very obstacle you wanted to avoid.

The same process happens in life: Focus on threats, and your brain constructs more fear. Focus on goals, and your brain constructs readiness, scanning the environment for resources and possibilities.

Here's the key: Predictions can be retrained. Each time you successfully ride a line you once thought impossible, your brain stores evidence: *I can.* Over time, this rewires your predictions about what's possible. Where you place your attention, you place your future.

Client Story: The Executive Staring at Rocks

One client, a senior leader, came to coaching because she felt stuck in a cycle of failure. Every project she took on, she said, "seems destined to go wrong." Bad decisions, bad outcomes, focus on the wrong things, her belief in her ability shaken. She was metaphorically "staring at the rocks."

When I asked her where she was focused, she claimed she was always worried about making more mistakes; her thoughts went to what could go wrong and what was likely to go wrong. We needed to work on shifting her focus. Instead of listing everything that could fail, I asked her to name one desired outcome for each project—sometimes as simple as, *I want my team to feel more aligned after this meeting. I want to get clarity on the next phase of this project.*

When her focus shifted, she began to look at what was going well and to focus on what she had control over. Eventually, her beliefs about herself and her capabilities aligned with better outcomes. She wasn't ignoring the challenges, and she was choosing the line she wanted to ride.

Your Coaching Reflection

Take a pause. Breathe. Reflect.

- Where is your attention going right now—toward obstacles or possibilities?
- Are you staring at the "rocks," or at the line you actually want to ride?
- What would shift if you focused more on what you want, instead of what you want to avoid?
- What's one belief you could upgrade from "I can't" to "I'm learning to"?

Tools: Training Your Focus

Name Your Line

Write a one-sentence outcome you want—not what you fear. Keep it visible.

Micro-Aim

Before meetings or tasks, ask: *What does the clean line look like for the next 30 minutes?*

Reframe in Motion

When facing a "big rock," shift self-talk from *I can't* to *I can test this in first gear.*

Visual Sweep

On trails or in tough conversations, sweep your eyes across options. Settle your gaze on where you want to go, not what you want to avoid.

Five-Count Reset

If you notice yourself spiraling, inhale for five, exhale for five, and consciously select a new focus.

Action: Align Your Line

For the next seven days, start each morning by choosing one clear focus—an outcome, a value, or a way of showing up. Write it down. Before your biggest "technical section" of the day, glance at it and commit to your line.

Closing Thought: Whatever we focus on expands. Our attention acts like a spotlight, amplifying the thoughts, emotions, and behaviors we concentrate on—whether helpful or hurtful. When we dwell on the obstacles presented in our lives, our energy and attention remain focused on limitations and problems. When we direct our attention toward possibilities, strengths, and intentional action, our energy fuels progress. Our focus is not passive; it's an active creator of momentum, shaping our experience and influencing our outcomes.

Energy flows where attention goes.
—JAMES REDFIELD

CHAPTER 9

Brake to Go Fast

Rest is not idleness, and to lie sometimes on the
grass under trees on a summer's day, listening to the
murmur of water, or watching the clouds float across
the sky, is by no means a waste of time.
—JOHN LUBBOCK

Life Lesson: Sometimes slowing down is the only way to speed up.

My Story: Training for the Century Ride

When I trained for my first century ride—100 miles on the bike—I was fired up and determined. My husband could cover the distance in about five to six hours. For me, it would take closer to all day. Determined to keep up, I pushed myself relentlessly—spinning classes, weight workouts, weekend rides. I piled on hours in the saddle, convinced that more was always better. But instead of feeling stronger,

I ended up with a sore back, heavy legs, aching shoulders, and a spirit that felt anything but joyful.

I trained myself straight into injury and burnout.

The irony? I had worked so hard to prepare for the longest ride of my life, but my approach nearly kept me from finishing it at all.

I had confused effort with effectiveness.

Without brakes, you can crash hard. Without rest, you burn out.

Cycling—and life—aren't built on constant grind. They're built on rhythm. Push and release. Work and recover. Stress and restoration. Rest is not wasted time. It's when your body consolidates strength, your brain integrates learning, and your energy stores refill. It's what makes the next effort possible. The brake isn't there to slow you down forever—it's what makes speed, safety, and endurance possible.

Neuroscience of the Ride: Rest, Prediction, and Recovery

From a **constructionist brain perspective**, your brain is constantly predicting what your body needs. When you chronically overtrain—or overwork—it predicts depletion, wiring your system toward exhaustion. Cortisol rises, attention narrows, and creativity collapses. The brain consolidates learning and strengthens neural connections during periods of rest.

Rest provides new sensory input: calm, safety, and replenishment. Sleep, downtime, and even mindful pauses signal to the brain that *we are safe enough to restore.* This recalibrates your "body budget," strengthens neural connections, and builds resilience. Just as muscles grow stronger in recovery, the brain wires itself most effectively when you pause.

Rest isn't laziness. It's construction time.

Client Story:
The Leader Who Wouldn't Stop Pedaling

One of my clients, a senior VP, prided herself on being the hardest worker in the room. Her calendar was wall-to-wall meetings, her evenings were filled with emails, and weekends blurred into weekdays. She was exhausted, but she believed stopping meant losing momentum.

I believe my client had succumbed to what I call "the myth of more." That is, somewhere along the way, many of us started confusing *more* with *better.* More hours, more meetings, more emails, more effort. We wear busyness like a badge of honor—as if exhaustion were proof of value and constant motion a sign of importance. In truth, busyness often masquerades as productivity. It gives us the illusion of progress while quietly eroding the clarity, creativity, and emotional stability that real personal effectiveness and leadership require. I've coached countless executives who believe they're being effective because their calendars are full, yet they're running on fumes—disconnected from their teams, their purpose, and even themselves.

The paradox is that restoration and reflection—the very things we tend to sacrifice first—are what allow us to operate at our best. Creativity doesn't happen in the grind; it occurs in the gaps. If there are no pauses or silences in music, it's just noise.

Slowing down isn't a weakness. It's wisdom. Some of the most effective leaders I've worked with understand that pausing is not quitting—it's calibrating. Rest and recovery aren't indulgences; they're investments in clarity, alignment with values, and sustainable performance.

It takes courage to step off the hamster wheel and say, "Enough. I choose to lead with presence, not just persistence."

I asked my client, "What if rest is not retreat, but fuel for the optimization of your time and effort?"

She agreed to experiment with this idea. She started by blocking 90 minutes of "white space" each Friday afternoon. No meetings. No emails. Just reflection, planning, or even staring out the window. She added a no-work-on-weekends policy. She recalibrated her meeting schedule to include breaks, so she had time to eat, review, and unwind. Within weeks, her team noticed she was calmer, clearer, and more creative. She noticed she had more energy for Monday mornings. She shared that she felt like she was more on point, rather than more exhausted.

Her performance hadn't dropped—in fact, it improved.

• ◈ •

Your Coaching Reflection

Take a pause. Breathe. Reflect.

- Where in your life are you "overtraining"—pushing without pause or recovery?
- How does lack of rest show up in your energy, creativity, or patience?
- What would it look like to honor rest as a vital part of your growth?
- What rhythms of recovery could you intentionally build into your week?

Tools: Braking with Intention

Schedule Recovery

Protect downtime the same way you protect key meetings. Treat rest as a strategy, not a weakness.

Follow the 90-Minute Rhythm

Work deeply for 90 minutes, then pause for 10–15. Your brain was built for cycles, not marathons.

Build Micro-Rest Rituals

Take a walk after lunch, step outside for fresh air, or journal for five minutes before bed.

Upgrade Your Sleep

Prioritize consistency, dark rooms, and tech-free wind-down routines. Sleep is your brain's #1 repair mechanism.

Reframe Rest as Training

Just like athletes taper their training regimen before big races, prepare yourself for big moments by resting more, not less.

Action: Check Your Brakes

This week, deliberately press one brake. Block one pause in your calendar, add one recovery ritual, or say no to one extra obligation. Then notice: How does slowing down actually help you speed up?

Closing Thought: Slowing down can help us because it creates the conditions for clarity, quality, and intentional action, rather than reactivity. During a pause, the brain shifts out of survival mode and into a state in which it can thoughtfully problem-solve, prioritize, and make connections more effectively. Slowing down also helps us notice assumptions, challenge automatic behaviors, and make choices that align with what truly matters. Paradoxically, the brief moments we take to breathe, reflect, and recalibrate often become the catalyst for faster progress, better results, and a sense of meaningful forward momentum.

Sometimes slowing down is the only way to speed up.
—UNKNOWN

CHAPTER 10

No Risk, No Reward

Darkness cannot drive out darkness;
only light can do that.
—Martin Luther King Jr.

Life Lesson: Risk is the price of truly living.

My Story: White Pass, Yukon Territory

I've had my share of frightening rides:

- On the first of my two Oregon Coast rides, near Redwoods National Park, a logging truck forced me into a ditch. I was saved from a big crash and bad injuries by my pannier bags.
- Once, on a trail ride near my house in Arizona, I crashed at over 20 miles an hour, broke my arm, smashed and cut my chin, had to walk four miles out of the park in immense pain, scared what my

full injuries would entail, still steering my bike to get to the car, and then spent six hours in the ER.

- My husband and I got lost on our first day riding in Spain (we didn't have GPS), had to keep riding into the dark, then ended up on a train, getting back to our hotel four hours later than we should have. And argued almost as fiercely as we pedaled over who got us lost.

But none of these incidents compares to what happened on White Pass.

I was riding from Whitehorse, Yukon Territory, into Alaska, climbing the legendary White Pass on the way to Glacier Bay National Park. My companion and I expected a tough ascent—long, steep, and, on this day, cold and rainy. We were prepared for any kind of weather, or so we thought.

The climb was grueling but manageable. The rain soaked us, but we had Gore-Tex gear, and on the way up, it kept me warm. At the summit, everything changed. On the windward side, the weather unleashed itself: wind shoved my bike across the road, rain cascaded in sheets, my hands went numb, I couldn't brake, and I hydroplaned uncontrollably. My body shook with cold; I could hear my teeth rattling.

Then I blacked out. Hypothermia had taken over.

What happened next, I only remember in fragments: being stuffed into a sleeping bag, lifted into the back of a van, waking up in a tiny border station hut.

I've been terrified of getting cold ever since. I overpack when I hike and bike to ensure I never go through that again. This fear of hypothermia is real, as is my choice to keep doing the things I love to do despite the risk.

That day could have ended my riding. Or at very least, I would be a fair-weather rider only. No one would have blamed me. But risk is part of living. I subscribe to the notion of "no risk, no reward."

Eventually, I got back on my bike—cautious, wiser, and more prepared. I now plan for contingencies and ride with greater awareness. But I still ride. Always with a backup jacket.

Fear thrives in darkness and uncertainty. What shrinks the fear isn't avoidance—it's clarity. Preparation, perspective, and courage are the lights that let us keep moving.

Life works the same way. You can try to avoid risk, but then you avoid growth, adventure, and joy. Or you can ride into it—equipped, supported, and willing to put yourself out there.

Neuroscience of the Ride:
Fear, Prediction, and Clarity

From a **constructionist perspective**, fear isn't simply a reflex—it's your brain making a prediction. When I crested White Pass, drenched and freezing, my nervous system had limited data: numb hands, violent wind, pooling water. My brain's model screamed: *This is life-threatening!* and shaped my experience of panic, tunnel vision, and eventual collapse. In other words, fear was not just the conditions—it was the story my brain assembled from those sensations.

Here's the good news: Constructionist neuroscience shows that we can train our brains to compose different predictions. Preparation (warmer gear, food, shelter plans), perspective (I've ridden through storms before), and trusted companions expand our body budget and give our brain new evidence. With this, our system predicts safety more often, even in harsh conditions.

Fear shrinks when clarity expands—because the brain stops imaging "danger everywhere" and starts predicting "challenge you can handle." Risk doesn't vanish, but your brain learns to ride through it with more options, not fewer.

Client Story: Facing the Unknown

One of my clients, a senior executive in healthcare, once described his leadership journey as "riding in the dark without lights." He had been promoted to a new role where he was suddenly responsible for decisions that impacted thousands of people. Overnight, what had once felt manageable became overwhelming. He told me he was staying awake night after night, afraid of "making the wrong call," self-describing his experience as being "stalled by fear." He second-guessed every decision, avoided risks, and clung to old habits because they felt safer.

The irony was that his hesitation became its own kind of risk. By avoiding bold decisions, he delayed progress on important initiatives, frustrated his team, and lost confidence in himself. Fear had narrowed his vision to only the worst-case scenarios.

In our coaching, we worked to bring in more clarity and have him feel more prepared for the random things that can happen in business or in life. Instead of trying to eliminate risk, he began to work toward increasing his understanding of the risks. He set up meetings to check in regularly with others as he built more confidence. In addition, he created "if/then" plans for key challenges and identified trusted peers he could lean on. Slowly, he found his footing again.

He shared with me: "The fear didn't go away. But once I put some contingencies in place, it stopped running the show."

Just like when I got back on the bike after my crash, he discovered that the way through fear wasn't avoidance—it was clarity, preparation, support, and courage.

· ◈ ·

Your Coaching Reflection

Take a pause. Breathe. Reflect.

- Where in your life are you avoiding risk that you could instead better prepare for?
- What (clarity, preparation, or support) would make the path less frightening?
- Which of your fears are real risks—and which are what I call False Evidence Appearing Real, or FEAR?
- What can you imagine might happen if you faced the fear that might make it worth it?

Tools: Riding Through Uncertainty

Name the Unknowns

Write down your fears. Separate real risks from imagined ones.

If/Then Planning

Reduce uncertainty by predeciding: *If X happens, then I will Y.*

Borrow Perspective

Ask someone who's been through it for wisdom. Their story adds clarity to your model.

Equip Yourself

Just as extra layers, lights, and gear reduce danger on the bike, build routines, rituals, and relationships that steady you when life gets stormy.

Action: Face Your Fear

This week, identify one place in your life where fear is holding you back. Add one light—clarify, prepare, or seek help—and notice how it changes your ride.

Closing Thought: Growth and opportunity rarely emerge without some form of risk-taking. Meaningful achievements seem to correlate with uncertainty and stepping into the unfamiliar. Risk doesn't have to be reckless. When we take thoughtful, intentional risks, we expand our capacity and discover new strengths. The reward isn't just the outcome—it's who we become in the process.

Only those who will risk going too far can possibly
find out how far one can go.
—HARRY CROSBY

Everyone Dies, Not Everyone Lives

It is not the length of life, but the depth of life.
—Ralph Waldo Emerson

Adventure has always been one of my top values, although, at age 62, my definition of adventure has shifted. Once, it was about maximizing mileage, steeper mountains, exotic destinations, or the technical challenge. Today, adventure feels simpler and, in many ways, richer.

Now, if I wake up and have time to get on my bike, it's a good day. Sometimes a great day. Sometimes I relearn what I've forgotten. Other times I simply take it all in—breathing gratitude into every moment I'm pedaling. I get to spend time in nature. I get to ride alongside my husband, often with our dog running happily nearby, or with friends who share this love of cycling. I get to feel strength and endurance in my body. I feel like I'm using my limited time well.

Cycling has given me such a consistent high and connected me so deeply to the planet, to others, and to myself.

Neuroscience of the Ride: Why Meaning Matters

Studies show that people who anchor their lives in *meaning and purpose* (not just pleasure) have healthier brains and bodies. Purpose reduces cortisol levels, strengthens immunity, and may even extend life-span. Adventure, connection, and joy aren't just nice ideas, they're survival strategies. When you choose to live fully, your brain literally functions better. Cycling has been my pathway to meaning, but neuroscience affirms: any practice that gives you autonomy, connection, and purpose rewires your brain toward resilience and fulfillment.

Everyone dies. But those who live with meaning leave behind not just memories—they leave behind neural ripples in every life they've touched.

The Deeper Lesson

My intent with this book is not about biking. It's about life. Cycling has been my teacher, my mirror, my compass. Through it, I've learned presence, resilience, joy, independence, courage, and the necessity of struggle.

It is my belief that truly living requires us to seek meaning in our limited days, to feel connected to the world and those around us, to savor the joy when we are experiencing it, to face the storms and hills because they amplify the easier days, and to chase what lights us up.

Whether you ever ride a bike or not, the invitation is the same:

- Find the thing that grounds you and lifts you at the same time.
- Let it connect you to yourself, to others, and to the world around you.
- Let it remind you that this moment—this breath, this ride, this life—is the adventure.

Your Invitation to Live:

- What does adventure mean to you at this stage of your life?
- Where are you settling for survival instead of truly living?
- What brings you consistent joy and connection? How can you do more of it?
- What small step could you take tomorrow to live, not just exist?

Every ride has an end. But while you are on it, you get to choose how fully you experience the journey—the climbs, the descents, the headwinds, the tailwinds, the joy and the ache of the ride itself.

From My Bike to You

If you've come this far with me, thank you. Thank you for riding alongside me through these stories, lessons, and reflections. Writing them has been another kind of journey—one filled with gratitude for every hill climbed, every road traveled, every scar earned, and every moment of joy on two wheels. I hope that something here sparked recognition in you—that you found yourself nodding, remembering, or imagining what living more fully might look like in your own life. You don't need a bike to live this way. You need courage to start, the presence to keep going, and gratitude to take it all in.

The road ahead is yours. May you ride it with strength, curiosity, and joy.

See you out there.

—Juliann Wiese

If interested in Keynote Presentations or Workshops,
contact Juliann at julzwiese@gmail.com

REFLECTIONS FROM THE RIDE

The following section is designed for readers to pause, reflect, and apply the insights from *Life Lessons on Two Wheels* to their own journey. Each reflection pairs the Life Lesson with the Action section—an invitation to bring the wisdom from the page into motion.

Chapter 1: Presence Is Precise

Life Lesson: The Power to Create Your Future Starts in the Present Moment

Reflection: What helps you come back to the moment when your mind drifts into worry or regret?

Action: What is happening right now? What can you be grateful for in this moment?

Chapter 2: Freedom and Choice

Life Lesson: Choose your own ride.

Reflection: What trade-offs are you willing to make for what you value most?

Action: Choose one area this week where you'll intentionally choose something that fills you up.

Chapter 3: Heartbreak Hill

Life Lesson: You can do hard things.

Reflection: Think of a recent uphill battle—what strengths did it reveal in you?

Action: Lean into your challenges with vigor and purpose.

Chapter 4: Obstacles and Distortions

Life Lesson: Comparison is the thief of joy.

Reflection: Where might pride, ego, and comparison be limiting your joy?

Action: Let go of something that frees you from comparison.

Chapter 5: Friction

Life Lesson: Conflict is a learning opportunity.

Reflection: Where are you avoiding tension that could be teaching you something?

Action: Approach one challenging conversation with curiosity instead of defensiveness.

Chapter 6: Shift Gears

Life Lesson: Change is hard, so is stagnation.

Reflection: Which change in your life needs patience rather than perfection?

Action: Choose one habit to shift. Expect discomfort—keep moving forward.

Chapter 7: Headwinds and Tailwinds

Life Lesson: Strength is built in the struggle, and joy is amplified by what we endure.

Reflection: What current headwind in your life might be strengthening you for what's next?

Action: Surface the bitter and the sweet so you can fully savor your life.

Chapter 8: Focus Creates Flow

Life Lesson: Attention is not neutral.

Reflection: Where is your attention going—and is it aligned with what matters most to you?

Action: Direct your focus toward what you want more of. Watch how your energy follows.

Chapter 9: Brake to Go Fast

Life Lesson: Sometimes slowing down is the only way to speed up.

Reflection: What does real restoration look like for you—not just a pause, but renewal?

Action: Add one intentional rest this week. Notice how it improves your clarity and pace.

Chapter 10: No Risk, No Reward

Life Lesson: Risk is the price of truly living.

Reflection: What dream or challenge are you avoiding because it feels risky?

Action: Choose one uncertainty and take a small, brave step toward it.

Final Reflection: Your Ride Ahead

- What did you discover about yourself through these lessons?
- Where do you want to shift your gears next?
- What "ride" are you ready to take on with more courage, compassion, and clarity?

REFERENCES

Attributed / Non-retrievable Quotes

Allen, J. L. (attrib.). Adversity does not build character, it reveals it.

Ford, H. (attrib.). If you always do what you've always done, you'll always get what you've got.

Ford, H. (attrib.). Whether you think you can or you think you can't—you're right.

Molière. (attrib.). The greater the obstacle, the more glory in overcoming it.

Roosevelt, F. D. (attrib.). A smooth sea never made a skilled sailor.

Whitman, W. (1855/1892). *Leaves of grass*. Happiness, not in another place but this place . . . not for another hour, but this hour.

Books

Barrett, L. F. (2017). *How emotions are made: The secret life of the brain*. Houghton Mifflin Harcourt.

Brown, B. (2010). *The gifts of imperfection*. Hazelden.

Damasio, A. (1994). *Descartes' error: Emotion, reason, and the human brain*. G. P. Putnam's Sons.

David, S. (2016). *Emotional agility: Get unstuck, embrace change, and thrive in work and life*. Avery.

Deci, E. L., & Ryan, R. M. (2017). *Self-determination theory: Basic psychological needs in motivation, development, and wellness.* Guilford Press.

Dillard, A. (1989). *The writing life.* Harper & Row.

Hebb, D. O. (1949). *The organization of behavior: A neuropsychological theory.* Wiley.

Holiday, R. (2014). *The obstacle is the way.* Portfolio.

Holiday, R. (2016). *Ego is the enemy.* Portfolio.

Kahneman, D. (2011). *Thinking, fast and slow.* Farrar, Straus and Giroux.

King, M. L., Jr. (1963). *Strength to love.* Harper & Row.

Lubbock, J. (1894). *The use of life.* Macmillan.

Lucado, M. (1994). *When God whispers your name.* Thomas Nelson.

Neff, K. (2011). *Self-compassion: The proven power of being kind to yourself.* William Morrow.

Parker, P. (2018). *The art of gathering: How we meet and why it matters.* Riverhead Books.

Redfield, J. (1993). *The Celestine Prophecy.* Warner Books.

Siegel, D. J. (2010). *Mindsight: The new science of personal transformation.* Bantam Books.

Thich Nhat Hanh. (1992). *Peace is every step.* Bantam.

Ury, W. (2007). *The power of a positive no: How to say no and still get to yes.* Bantam Books.

Articles / Papers

Gino, F., Di Stefano, G., Pisano, G. P., & Staats, B. R. (2016). Learning by thinking: How reflection improves performance. *Organizational Science, 27*(3), 623–641.

Grant, A. M., & Parker, S. K. (2009). Redesigning work design theories: The rise of relational and proactive perspectives. *Academy of Management Annals, 3*(1), 317–375.

Gruber, M. J., Gelman, B. D., & Ranganath, C. (2014). States of curiosity modulate hippocampus-dependent learning via the dopaminergic circuit. *Neuron, 84*(2), 486–496.

Kahneman, D., & Tversky, A. (1979). Prospect theory: An analysis of decision under risk. *Econometrica, 47*(2), 263–291.

Speeches / Hard-to-source items

Anthony, S. B. (1893). Happiness is independence [Speech excerpts/paraphrase].

ACKNOWLEDGMENTS

Writing a book is never a solo ride—it's a peloton. I owe deep gratitude to the companions who drafted beside me, cheered me on, and reminded me to keep pedaling when the hills grew steep. To my family: to my dad, whose love of cycling sparked my own and has inspired every ride I've taken; to my mom, who modeled entrepreneurship and independence; and to my husband, John—my steadfast partner on and off the bike. You've shared countless miles, adventures, and detours with me.

To my oldest friends and cycling buddies—you've shared the Oregon Coast, Tuscany, Colorado climbs, and so many other unforgettable roads. You've given me not just camaraderie but perspective, laughter, and belonging. A special thanks to my dear friends and fellow riders, Jodi and Jim Tompkins, whose companionship on two wheels and in life has been a constant source of encouragement and joy. Also to Jan and Rich Leighton, the biking adventures with you were always memorable, fun-filled and inspiring.

To my former boss and incredible mentor, Barb Patterson: none of this would have been possible without your steady nudges toward independence, purpose, and meaning. To my friend and coach, Amy Van Court: your wisdom, support, and encouragement will always be treasured. To my friend and colleague, Karyn Edwards, PhD,

MCC: thank you for your time, honesty, friendship, and helpful insight. I often ask myself, "What would Karyn do here?"—and that voice keeps me grounded and true. To my coaching colleagues, mentors, and clients—thank you for entrusting me with your stories, challenges, and dreams. Every conversation has been a chance to learn, grow, and refine the lessons in these pages. You are the true coauthors of this book.

To the teachers and thinkers whose work shaped my own—your research and wisdom provided the frameworks that connected my lived experience with the science of how we grow. To my editor, early readers, and those who pushed me gently back on the bike when I doubted I could finish, your guidance, feedback, and belief made this book stronger, clearer, and truer. And finally, to every rider who has ever waved from the road, shared a draft, offered a snack at a rest stop, or encouraged me to climb one more hill—you embody the spirit of community and generosity that cycling, and life itself, are about.

This book is for all of you who ride—whether on two wheels or through the ups and downs of everyday life. Thank you for being part of this journey.

Juliann Wiese is a Master Certified Coach (MCC) and executive consultant with over 3,000 hours of coaching experience. For more than a decade, she has worked with leaders, teams, and organizations across industries to help them build resilience, authenticity, and impact. A lifelong cyclist, Juliann has been riding for over 50 years—from childhood rides in Banff, Alberta, to century rides in New Mexico, to adventures in Ireland, Spain, and Italy. Along the way, she discovered that the lessons learned on two wheels—about courage, presence, ego, and joy—are the very lessons that shape a meaningful life. When she's not coaching or writing, you'll find her on a bike path with her husband, grinning wide enough to catch a few bugs in her teeth.